ALEXIS *has a* STORY *to* TELL YOU

Princess Alexis Beloved

Alexis Has A Story to Tell You
Copyright © 2024 Princess Alexis Beloved

All rights reserved. No part of this book, "Alexis Has A Story to Tell You," may be reproduced, distributed, or transmitted in any form or by any means, including photocopying, recording, or other electronic or mechanical methods, without the prior written permission of the author, except in the case of brief quotations embodied in critical reviews and certain other noncommercial uses permitted by copyright law.

Scriptures marked KJV are taken from the KING JAMES VERSION (KJV): KING JAMES VERSION, public domain.
Scripture taken from the New King James Version®. Copyright ©1982 by Thomas Nelson. Used by permission. All rights reserved.

Scripture quotations marked (NIV) are taken from the Holy Bible, New International Version®, NIV®. Copyright © 1973, 1978, 1984, 2011 by Biblica, Inc.™ Used by permission of Zondervan.

All rights reserved worldwide. www.zondervan.com. The "NIV" and "New International Version" are trademarks registered in the United States Patent and Trademark Office by Biblica, Inc.™.

Unless otherwise indicated, all Scripture quotations are taken from the Holy Bible, New Living Translation, copyright © 1996, 2004, 2015 by Tyndale House Foundation. Used by permission of Tyndale House Publishers, Carol Stream, Illinois 60188. All rights reserved.
For permission requests to use stories or quotes from this book, email the author at alexisbeloveddd@gmail.com

Published by:
Eleviv Publishing Group
Xenia, OH 45385
info@elevivpublishing.com
www.elevivpublishing.com
ISBN: (HC) 978-1-952744-83-9
    (E-book) 978-1-952744-84-6

Printed in the United States of America

DEDICATION

This book is dedicated to God, the Son (Jesus), and The Holy Spirit because I survived and made it this far through them. I would like to extend my dedication to the ones who feel how I once felt—believing God has no use for them. To everyone who has a story to tell, whether you've been a victim of abuse, rape, suicidal thoughts, depression, and more, know that from reading this, your deliverance has come.

Today, in the Name of Jesus, YOU have been SET FREE. To Apostle Queen Belemzy, my destiny helper, I dedicate this to you for always obeying God and never giving up on me. Showing me what it's like to be loved with the true Love of God from the way you love me.

You have been a breath of fresh air. Your teaching, preaching, and leading by example have shown me what it means to truly give your life to Jesus Christ.

To friends and family who have been by my side or parted ways, you all have made my life an experience worth writing about. God bless you. I love you all with the Love of God.

ACKNOWLEDGMENTS

I want to take this time to thank Jesus Christ for sacrificing His life for me to be saved.

Apostle Queen Belemzy, thank you for not only accepting the call of God but also allowing Jesus to use you to bring me to Him. Being the greatest gift of many answered prayers—my family, QBM-SOP Family, and my friends for all your support and love. I also want to thank my college professor, Professor Aronovitz, because he told me I would be a great writer and even write books someday. I also want to thank my parents and abusers because of you all; I have a story to tell. And for that, I am grateful.

TABLE of CONTENTS

INTRODUCTION

CHAPTER ONE
The Genesis of Princess Alexis Beloved... *10*

CHAPTER TWO
My Dreams Growing up... *38*

CHAPTER THREE
The Power of Prayer... *41*

CHAPTER FOUR
Repenting and Giving My Life to Christ... *45*

CHAPTER FIVE
A New Creature... *83*

CHAPTER SIX
Telling my Story... *89*

FINAL WORDS
A Message from my Heart... *99*

YOUR STORY CAN BECOME A GREAT MESSAGE

INTRODUCTION

"Oh yes, You shaped me first inside, then out; You formed me in my mother's womb. I thank You, High God—You're breathtaking! Body and soul, I am marvelously made! I worship in adoration— what a creation! You know me inside and out, You know every bone in my body; You know exactly how I was made, bit by bit, how I was sculpted from nothing into something. Like an open book, You watched me grow from conception to birth; all the stages of my life were spread out before You, The days of my life all prepared before I'd even lived one day." Psalms 139:13-16 MSG

Hello. My name is Alexis Beloved. I'm here to share with you the most important events of my life that I once considered confidential. Maya Angelou once said, *"There is no greater agony than bearing an untold story inside you."*

Everyone's life is intended to be different. It comes with many trials and difficulties, some moments of pure happiness and others you wish to erase from your mind. For me, the bad often outweighed the good, and this is a story of how far God has brought me.

Coming from a place of brokenness, I had to learn to give God full access to fix what I thought could never be repaired, which was me. I endured many things until I felt God knew I couldn't take it anymore. When I encountered Queen Belemzy Ministries—School of Power, Jesus began to fill that emptiness. I learned that my story is my message, no matter how hard it is to tell. This is a quote from my Apostle herself: *"Everybody has something they have to go through so that they can have a story to tell."- Apostle Queen Belemzy.*

Growing up, I tried so hard to hide what I was embarrassed to speak up about. I hated myself for it. I wanted to act as if it never happened. Being in a family that made me feel unwanted gradually made me lean towards God more. Although I didn't lean towards God at all in the beginning but instead I prayed to God many times to die just because I felt that being alive was a burden. If God didn't allow this to happen, I wouldn't know that regardless of whether anyone loves me, He will always love me.

On August 13th, 2023, at 11:40 pm, I received this assignment from God through my Apostle (Apostle Queen Belemzy) that it was time to author my book. I was also instructed to stay at her house for seven days. For one of those seven days, I fasted dry with no food or water; although it was hard, by the grace of God, I was given an angel named Leo to help me write this book. Towards the end of the book, I prayed, asking God how He wanted the cover and the title to look. Through a vision, my Apostle saw exactly how my cover should look, and after telling me, I obeyed. I immediately had to order clothes from Amazon to bring the vision to life. Then God whispered the title of my book to her. With that, I was so happy.

I am truly blessed to be around someone who hears from God. Throughout this process, my Apostle has been my biggest supporter and guidance.

If I were to be completely honest, writing this book was an emotional roller coaster because, through the process, I realized how far God has brought me. Most of the time, writing, I felt like I was reliving each moment. Throughout the sufferings, I realized God never took His hands off me. Even as I write this, I'm just getting overwhelmed with gratitude.

Today, I am reminded of God's love for me; He sent His only Begotten Son to die for me. I thought I was unworthy, which I know I am, but He looked beyond my unworthiness and counted me worthy. I consider it an honor and a privilege to write the story God created me to have. This is the Beginning of the Story, I have to tell you.

The GENESIS of PRINCESS ALEXIS BELOVED

"Before I formed you in the womb I knew you, before you were born I set you apart; I appointed you as a prophet to the nations." Jeremiah 1:5 NIV

My mom was in high school when she got pregnant with me. As God willed it, I was born in Pennsylvania in the winter of December 1997. After many trials of attempting abortion, the third time became the final straw, because it didn't work. Finding out about the pregnancy my grandfather was not happy; in fact, he was pretty aggressive when he found out she was pregnant. My mom had to jump out of her room window to go to her aunt's house for safety. Her unplanned pregnancy became such a big issue between both families and a lot of suggestions about keeping me or giving me up because not having me wasn't an option anymore. No one agreed with anything.

Looking back now, a part of me can understand the trauma my mom must have been through at that age- getting pregnant and going through so much disappointment and rejection from her family. Having to make such a life-changing decision to have and keep a child when you're just a child yourself. Watching your friends partying, going to prom, and doing so much more can be very traumatizing. She was just a kid.

For a long time, I didn't look at how they would have felt or how the trauma would have caused her a lot of pain. The thought of how people even looked at my dad as well. What he would have probably felt. Personally, I have no clue because I never really got the chance to ask.

While she was still pregnant, she was given the choice of giving me up to a family in New York, and she turned it down. She said if she could have the baby, she could take care of it.

After having me, she returned to school and had no choice but to ensure she came home on time to care for me. So she worked so hard and then finally moved out on her own.

I would visit my dad sometimes until it was finally taken to court. So, for a little while, I didn't see my dad. I have lived in a custody battle for almost a quarter of my childhood, and it wasn't easy at all. I felt like I had to choose sides. At times, when it got rough, I wished I could just be with my dad. Of course, I knew who my dad was for a while, but there was a time when I began to forget him, even with the dreams.

As a child, I always expressed myself. From an adult point of view, I talked a lot. Before getting into trouble, I always said the first thing on my mind. After that, I became shy. Toys helped build my imagination with everything going on. My memory was very vivid. I remembered the relationships my mom was in before when I was in kindergarten.

When she got this other apartment, I'm sure she intended to make a better life for us on her own, but like I said before, things don't always go as planned. I don't know how many apartments we had before getting the nicer one. I loved it there. I had my own room. It was just the two of us at first. I went to school, and she went to work, but she did work a lot. With that, I learned to do things on my own. I often stayed in my room; I even learned to use the microwave. I had an easy bake oven, so I thought I was a chef. She had a slight tempter, so I always tried to stay out of her way. Being at peace, I loved school, drawing, singing, and just being in my own world. Slowly, everything began to change for me.

WHEN TRAUMA TRIED TO TAKE OVER ME

"Consider it a sheer gift, friends, when tests and challenges come at you from all sides. You know that under pressure, your faith-life is forced into the open and shows its true colors. So don't try to get out of anything prematurely. Let it do its work so you become mature and well-developed, not deficient in any way. " James 1:2-4 MSG

They say trauma comes to you through various experiences, life-changing and sometimes earth-shattering events; those events define you and change you. There are strategic methods the enemy uses to entrap and enslave those he's set his sight on. Often, abuse is a gateway for the devil, and did he use it to enslave me! My life-changing moment was before I turned 6. I don't remember when, but her younger brother moved in with us (his name starts with an M). That's when everything became a blur. I couldn't clearly remember when it was just me and my mom because he was always there. I've always known my mom to want to help people, especially her family; it was her passion. It was a different energy when it came to me.

Being a single parent, she was barely home. So, for a while, I was always alone with him. When you're alone, it creates room for many things to happen, definitely when you are just a child.

My mother's younger brother (M) started molesting me when I was just 5 to 6 years of age. Molestation can be a tricky word because the meaning seems so broad, but to be forthright and fully transparent, I was raped anally by my mother's younger brother (M) as a little girl, which means that he used his private in my anus to satisfy himself. This happened daily, sometimes twice daily, depending on how long my mom worked. It was like clockwork. The worst part is that he made it seem like a good thing, and it was also a secret. You know how older people tell kids it's just a secret? To him, it was a game. He made me believe that what he was doing to me was helping me, as if it was an honor for him to choose me. At that time, I didn't think anything of it. I had to keep most of this in my head because he told me that if I spoke up about it, I would get in trouble, not him.

I hated getting in trouble, and I always got into trouble with my mom, whether I did anything or not, because I was available.

This was the time that I started hating how I looked. My body, how it was shaped, and even my face. He always complimented me on how beautiful I looked, and the more he said it, the more I hated hearing it. That's when depression began. I remembered a lot; I knew a lot, but I stopped trying to make sense of everything happening. I didn't even want to speak quickly, which made it a habit of hiding things out of fear. I feared people would not believe me even if I spoke up, so I retreated within and allowed him to do whatever he wanted. It's a feeling of not knowing how to feel, but what you feel is discomforting, and you have no clue how to fix it. For an entire year, this man, my mom's brother, molested me. For some reason, I always thought I spoke to my mom about it, but she never believed me and was in denial. I didn't even know how to express myself. I would even shut down when I had something important to say; I would just say never mind or stop talking. It happened for so long that I even struggled with school where even my teacher was bullying me, so I stopped doing my work. I couldn't speak up because my mom believed everyone over me.

When my mom found out about the bullying, she

didn't believe me until she saw the teacher in action, but then I was already beaten by my mom for it. All of these, the molestation, the bullying, and the physical abuse, were happening simultaneously. When her older sister came from Liberia to visit us, she tried to defend me, and that day, the beating was worse. Her older sister (P) sensed what was happening the first few days of being in the house. By the second or third week, she had watched my every move; she knew something was up. She even yelled at me and blamed me a lot; on one of those days, she asked me to lie down so she could check my private area to be sure. When she found out I was being sexually abused, she called her brother right away and started yelling and saying that what he was doing could get them sent back, not just him, but her too, back to Africa.

    I remember that day as clear as day. I was still lying on the floor with my pants down when she made that call. She even insisted that it was my fault it was happening. (P) said that American kids are so sneaky. She made it clear to me that if I told my mom about this, it would only be me who would get that beating, not them, and that my mom would be furious at me. From that, I knew which side she was on. Not too long after that, she started touching me. I only remember her doing it one time, and even after warning her brother, he continued to molest me. It didn't stop him; it was more of an encouragement. It felt like they were a team. The older I got, the more it happened with different people, family, friends, and cousins. All these events occurred when my mom was at work.

Growing up, she always left me places; my dad left me in various places, even though I wasn't with him often. I had to learn to fend for myself and be my own protector. I built this wall for so long that I never understood how to take it down. Sometimes, I wonder if those walls are entirely down now. I won't lie; learning to fend for myself was the hardest. I wished I had never been born so many times. I always felt so alone. If I didn't protect myself, who would? I didn't think of God or wonder if He existed; I was six. I just always felt I didn't belong here. It didn't take a lot to make me happy. I'm still like that now.

Whenever my mom would find love, I would get a break. I would feel a sense of love, and then when that relationship was over, we would return to square one. I remember when she met my stepdad, and I was so happy for her. I could tell the love was real. I finally got to see my dad again, which made me happy. My stepdad was there frequently, and then my dad took me often, so there was no room for me to be molested. I would finally get a break. My stepdad was truly there for my mom. Even when she was sick, he was always there for her. He was good to her, and I got to see that. I didn't always see her being treated well, so I was happy for her. We had a lot of traumatic experiences with boyfriends, and it was a lot; some were good, and others were just terrible.

I always felt that if she were happy, it would make room for me to be happy, too. My stepdad (M) started to feel like another father to me. As in love as they were, they were ready to move in together, which meant moving to another state or town where he lived. This meant leaving me behind with her siblings to finish school. It was a time when the numbness kicked in. You can just begin to imagine how I felt. Just when I thought it was all over. I was left behind. I felt the impact of her leaving me. I still know exactly how I felt.

Although her brother wasn't there as often, I felt so alone. Yes, I was happy because him not being there meant that I wouldn't be getting molested. But I was also left with someone who didn't care about me. So I played outside most of the time alone because my aunt always had someone over, so she never really paid attention to me anyway. One day, I was outside, playing with another girl who lived in the apartment complex—drawing with chalk on the ground when this guy came and ran me over with his bike. The girl was gone. It was just me, and he kept going. As a kid, I just felt like it could only get worse from here. I just went inside.

Instead of getting worse, some people came to the door within a few days of that incident. They were dressed in all white from head to toe. Two men and one lady, but the lady did most of the talking. They were so tall, with a glow on them, I couldn't even see their faces. They were inviting us to Church, and that was when I learned about Jesus Christ and that He existed. I learned that He could save me. We didn't go there for long because soon after that, I got to move in with my mom and stepdad. I still remember the first time I stepped into that church. I don't know if it was just the children's department, but it looked like an all-white room. It was beautiful and pure, really Heavenly. For some reason, I know the three people that came to the door were angels. It only became apparent once I got older. I had no clue God was looking out for me even then.

Once school ended and I finished 1st grade, I moved with them, and it was closer to my stepdad's side of the family. I was so excited. I met my cousins, started in a new school, made new friends, and had a new family. The shocking part is that when I was much younger, my stepdad's aunt's house was where my dad used to drop me off when he had me at times. The literal meaning is that this is a small world. Some of them, I could sense, had different intentions, and some I felt just wanted to be my cousins.

Although I had to grow up fast, being around them made me feel my age. The part I didn't like about getting older was that the punishments were intense. I felt that I wasn't being disciplined like everyone else. It always felt drastic and overbearing, as if I was just a stress reliever. I became the punching bag even if I didn't do anything or wasn't at fault. So, I blamed myself a lot for still being here. Sometimes, I thought the beating would be so bad that she could possibly kill me one day. If she did, deep down, I felt life for them would be easier.

The moment puberty hit, I was excited at first because every kid began to hit their peak, and I wasn't growing anywhere. Then, when it kicked in, I wished for everything to go away. It felt like it was more of a curse than a blessing. I didn't know anything besides what I learned in school. I wasn't taught many things and had to learn independently when it came to periods, pads, and hygiene. Sex education was a taboo. The most I got were talks like, "If you get pregnant, I'll send you to Africa and cut all communication with you, then bring someone else here in your name." Quite frankly, sex wasn't even on my mind. Many times, my mom did accuse me of being sexually active.

One day, when I was at my stepdad's aunt's house, she sent my cousin (boy) and me across the street to get something for her because she was the family's cook. Something was different this time because they usually would bring what she wanted, but she sent us there, and when we went, I knew something was off, and I couldn't tell what it was. But I had a feeling. Before I even moved there, I went to stay with one of my mom's family friends during the night, and I was raped there. So when we were sent there, I got this feeling in my stomach, and I knew it wouldn't end well. We were in for a field day. I became the project guinea pig for the guy and his friends to learn about. I was in elementary school then, and my family friend, not my cousin, and his friends were in high school. I don't remember what happened to my cousin who went with me, but he was touched inappropriately as well.

After that day, we were never the same. I was just in second grade. Their little experiment stopped when my stepdad's aunt came and opened the garage door, and told us to leave. I was still on the floor, with no underwear, and just looking at her. While the others just looked at me, it felt like that was their plan. I never said anything about it. I just pretended like it never happened. I just knew I could never be around them again like I was that day. Just like how I pushed everything away, I had to do the same with that. After that summer, when we were in our place.

After making this big move, there was trouble in paradise. The home became very toxic, where they were arguing a lot and breaking things. I couldn't handle any of it. Having been in a similar situation with my mom before, it was just too much. My mom then found out my stepdad was cheating. He left, and after he left, my mom blamed me for it. That's when

I knew this relationship they had was bigger than me. I was getting blamed a lot for everything, even their breakup. One morning, she woke up frustrated, and she beat me badly before school just because one of my dresses fell off the hangers. After she dropped me off at school, the first person to see my bruised arm was the crossing guard. This bruise was big. It was a little after my wrist to the middle of my arm. Although the crossing guard saw it first before me and my mom left the house after the beating, I felt the pain intensifying, but I ignored it and didn't look at it.

The crossing guard (she was black, so she knew what happened) told me how to avoid getting asked many questions because I would have to get ice for it to go down. It did not go as planned. When I went down to the nurse, my teacher had already called the nurse. She stated that another student said to her that she saw my bruises and that the bruises were from my mom beating me. I planned on saying that my arm got smashed into a door. That's the story I intended to tell her, and it didn't go as planned. We went through a lot of tests and questions throughout that day. I barely went back to class because, before I knew it, they already called child protective services. I had no clue. I just kept lying to cover up for my mom. I wasn't even worried about the ice anymore; I knew I was about to get in trouble. Before I could even think, they set up an African American social worker so that I could feel comfortable enough to talk to her.

She told me that she understood what I was going through. She was there before, and I don't know what it was about her, but I was convinced. Mind you, I was only in third grade. It became a massive thing. During the investigation, they didn't call her instantly; they called her later while my arm was healing. When she finally got the call, she started calling the whole family and telling them what I did but never apologized. She even took me to Church; they prayed all night because of me. I was praying for the CPS to come because I was tired of everything while they were busy praying against it happening. So, after the prayer, the social workers never came. One night, she came to my room, and she was crying. For the first time, she apologized to me. She told me she would never put anything above me again. Like genuinely love me.

Eventually, my stepdad returned, and they got back together. However, I no longer had the same bond with him; everything was different. During that period, my dad wanted full custody of me. My dad wasn't always as consistent as he claimed to be. Due to that, he wouldn't get full custody. He never even showed up in court. Eventually, my mom won and got full custody.

My parents made arrangements that allowed me to see my dad and half-siblings, but sometimes, I wasn't allowed to see them. Even with the arrangements, my mom stopped them often. My parents would always argue, and the bigger the arguments, the less likely I would see them. I enjoyed seeing my siblings and loved being around them; it was like an escape from the troubles at home. It made me feel like I wasn't going through what I was going through. If they only knew, they helped make my childhood a little less scary, especially my older sister. I could tell she loved me, like her own personal doll.

When I stopped going to my dad for summers, I started going to her sister's for summer holidays, which I hated. For some reason, I always felt like when I went over there, I was going to be a slave because she was very mean to me all the time. There was a time when she slapped me in front of her friends because I didn't cook enough rice. There were times that I felt like she put me in harm's way, knowing that she and her brother did things to me when I was younger. This one summer, she left me in the house with him, and he tried to rape me again. And when this happened, I had to defend myself. I fought him off. I didn't care if I wasn't strong enough; I decided to fight.

And I remember that day so clearly because so many things happened. When I was trying to fight him off, he laughed at me. He paused, then laughed. He said, "Oh, you think you're tough now?" Once he said that, he just left me alone. And I felt like the moment he touched me; he left me with the same kind of spirit he had. That made me want to rebel, and I wanted them to pay for what they did to me, but I had nobody to stand up for me. I wanted her son to go through the same thing I felt, but I couldn't go through with it. I knew I would never be able to forgive myself if I did. I had to think who would believe me now. God saved me from making the worst life decision, and I almost went through with it.

Nothing changed, but some days were good. Those were the days I cherished the most. There was no consistency with anything good; it never lasted. I used to think it was because I was an only child. So, I always hoped and prayed for me to have children. But when she did get pregnant, there were just miscarriages instead. I wondered why God kept taking them away when they were so close. I wanted to be the one that He took away instead. It made no sense to me for me to be in this world if my parents saw me as a burden. When it came to my dad, I knew he didn't care anyway; he had so many kids, and I was just another one.

I couldn't even trust people. Even when I would hear someone tell me they love me, much of that insecurity started from home. I don't even remember my mom telling me she loves me, and although my dad said it, I still felt that he didn't mean it. My mom always told people that she wanted me to fear her. I would never say I was a perfect child. I was far from it. I made so many mistakes, either on purpose or actual mistakes. Even with it being on purpose, it was sometimes too much. I just didn't want to be a burden. Oftentimes, I felt like that. I wasn't even allowed to go anywhere unless it was with them or when it was with friends, probably once for my birthday and the rest with them. When I did go out, I took advantage of it. I had to make the most of it.

When we discovered I needed glasses from elementary school, my mom felt I was lying, so I only got glasses once I got to high school, which was when my eyesight got terrible. I didn't like sitting in the front, so in addition, with my grades being bad, I couldn't see. In middle school, I began to do very well. I remember being on the honor roll in eighth grade more than once throughout that year. Then, when I got to high school, I tried a little bit because I started doing sports from seventh to eighth grade, which I loved. So, I continued in High school. When other kids' parents came to see their games, I made it seem like I didn't care. It bothered me. I did track and also volleyball; I loved being in sports. I've only played volleyball for one year, and then after that, it was track all the way. I played basketball for a day, but it didn't work out. Although I never said it, having your parents when you're involved in anything in school matters. The track became like another getaway from reality. It became such a distraction I was failing my classes badly. As any parent would, my mom said the track must be on hold until I get my grades together. I didn't listen to that. I stopped when I got injured and then brought my grades up.

The year after, I had to repeat a class or two in high school—one in 10th grade and one in my senior year. My mom was unhappy, and I did not hear the end of it. She would call me all the names in the book: stupid, foolish goat, and many more. Many times, I got cursed out like that. I thought it was normal. She would say that my dad doesn't even really care about me, that he has other kids that he cares about, and that I'm not the kid that he cares about; most of those times when I got in trouble, I got threatened to get sent to Liberia, one of the main reasons why I feel like I didn't want to go. I just stayed out of the way often, which meant being in my room.

    What kept my mind at ease was listening to music. Or even drawing, even made me reorganize often that I never finished. I felt like I could hide within the music. It was like an escape for me for as long as I can remember. I always like how I feel listening to a song. I could see visions of living within the sound. With singing, I felt like I could do so much with my voice, but I had stage fright. I was so afraid of rejection, thinking people wouldn't like my voice. I was always humming if I wasn't sitting in front of the TV drawing. I tried to hide it, but it was a part of me. Sound always did something for me. It made me feel as though I was in a different world.

In school, I made friends very quickly. Many people knew me, but that also had to do with us moving a lot and going to different school districts, being in different schools, being around different crowds, and knowing all diverse types of people. Many people knew my name even when I didn't know their names. One thing I was famous for was the fact that I was always getting in trouble with my mom. My teachers knew my phone would get taken away when I got in trouble. My mom wouldn't talk to me. I barely had problems with kids at school, but with her, it was like high school at home. Let me give you this scenario. If I paid for lunch and she wasn't talking to me, I better not even ask. I would not get lunch money for that day, so I would not eat lunch. There was an incident in middle school when I started track, which I was excited about.

I have no clue why, but we went food shopping, and I was like, OK, I'm going to get yogurt. I wanted to be so healthy. I'm not sure why, but my mindset is still so funny. The moment the yogurt was placed in the fridge, that's all I ate. I ate it for breakfast, lunch, and dinner and finished it within three days. She told me I shouldn't touch the refrigerator again, and I got in trouble to the point where she wasn't even giving me lunch money again. I did not eat at home or school for a week while running track. I started getting skinny from then. I even had friends who would share snacks with me so I wouldn't pass out at track practice.

Then, there was a day I was so hungry I went to take a croissant out of the refrigerator. After a week of no real food, I started praying and cried to God. I cried. I felt like He hated me. While crying to God, she joked after they ordered food, asking if I wanted to eat. I never went downstairs that day for the Chinese food because I felt she was mocking me, although I don't think she thought I would listen to her and not eat. That's how afraid of her I was. I tiptoed around her most of the time because food was one of her main issues with me. She always talked about my weight being up and down.

Then, there was a time she accused me of taking soup out of the freezer. She said I removed some of the meat I wanted and returned the soup to the deep freezer. She insisted that's what I did. I later discovered that she was the one who took it out to give it to one of her friends. That day, I was on my own. She called her husband to come and inspect the frozen soup after hitting me in my head with it. Just for him to agree with her that the food looks tampered with. I just wanted to go to my room. I thought that was it. She had already made up her mind that she was about to beat me for it, and for some reason, she decided to beat me near the stairs.

Before I could even think, I was on the floor, and she was beating me. It was just getting too much. She went ahead to take her foot and put it on my neck. The moment she did that, I was over it. I said this lady is not about to kill me. When I grabbed her foot, she started yelling that I wanted to fight her, so her husband came and said it's enough. When he arrived, I was already off the floor at my room door, closing the door. I was in disbelief, like, wow, she almost killed me. The next day, she apologized, but it was too late. The damage was already done. I felt every inch of the beating on top of the workouts from the track. This was the second time in my whole life she ever apologized to me. There were a lot of times when the beatings were beyond extreme.

I've been peppered many times *(when they boil habanero peppers and mash it up, putting it in your private area and your eyes, and you had to stay hours with it on)*. I had to pump tire *(African punishment when you put your fingers in your ears or hold your ears and squat until they say stop)*. I pumped tire all night before, then went to school. Also, before school, I was always getting peppered. The crazy part is the beatings never stopped regardless of how old I got; it just got worse. Can you imagine I was getting beaten in college? Yes, I got the worst beating of my life when I was in college. My biological father's mother gave me money to shop for clothes as a gift in college. Instead, I used some of it for school because I knew at the time we were paying out of pocket.

Eventually, I did use some for shopping, but this money was not in my possession; even though I was in college, she kept this money in her room in a drawer. I just knew where it was. So when I wanted to go shopping, I took the money from that drawer because it was mine. One morning, she woke up very angry, but for me, this was a day I was just thrilled. I don't know what happened. I just woke up happy and was cleaning up my room, minding my business. She bolted into my room, asking me where the money was. The drawer wasn't empty, and I explained to her what I used the money for recently. Which I always did when I was using it, but I explained again.

So she left the room and said that when she came back, she wanted to see everything I bought with the money, so I said, "OK." I got all the clothes I had bought and put them on the bed. I didn't think anything of it, so I continued cleaning. I was using the broom when she suddenly came in and started yelling. I put the broom to the side. The broom had metal on the inside but was covered with plastic. She took the broom and instantly started beating me with it. That broom broke, and she continued beating me with it when my pinky finger started gushing blood. That's when she stopped, and everybody came into the room. At that time, I went into shock. At some point, I was sitting in blood because my leg had already been bleeding for a while.

They rushed me to the bathroom. We saw that my head was bleeding as my pinky on my right hand, my pointing finger on my left, and lastly, my right leg had the biggest cut because of how I was sitting; it was hard to see it at the time. I remember seeing a lot of blood, and I started shaking. My stepdad was telling my mom that things like this could make her lose her license, and when she heard that, she fainted. The moment she did that, whatever pain I was feeling, whatever shock I was in, I came out of it. I was confused as to why she was the one who was fainting when I was the one who almost died. I want to fight her. I already knew I was not going to the hospital. So that day, she took my phone when she left the house and ensured I iced my head because I lost hair. Besides that, she felt like I would call the police on her, so she took my phone. We had to do temporary stitches on my leg mainly because the wound was deep.

She didn't want me to go to the hospital, and then, if they asked what happened, we wouldn't know what to say. After that incident, she became so nice to me. She was so nice, everybody became confused. For a while, I limped because I couldn't bend my knee all the way, or else the stitches would rip open. There was a time when we had to check to ensure there was no metal. Out of nowhere, I felt something scraping my leg like something was in there. I had to lie to people and say I fell. The ones that knew knew. I even lied to my pastor at that time. I was getting so tired of lying to protect someone that could kill me eventually. Defending the one that constantly reminds me that I was a mistake to her. I was more tired than I'd ever been. I just wanted God to end it; if He wasn't going to, I wanted to end it myself.

Even though I was going to Church, I still wasn't

happy. I was so depressed, suicidal, and drained, but I didn't want to show it or let people know. I spent my whole life pretending as if nothing ever happened to me. It gave the impression that I had no meaning in life or storyline. I learned to drive from my cousin, but it was also a way for me to adapt to other habits. I drank alcohol, but not as one would think. I knew I could consume a lot, so I wasn't a huge fan of it. It scared me that no matter how much I consumed, I wouldn't get drunk; I even started smoking weed; the number of times I did, I can count on one hand. When I turned 21, God told me not to drink again. My God, it was an adventure. I was laughing nonstop, and trust me, nothing was funny. Someone could drop something, and I would laugh. It wasn't obvious that's what I was doing because I loved laughing around my cousins. That's all we ever did. The big change was if they could smell or see our eyes, that would expose us. It was not for me.It became a habit for me not to sleep often; I was always up. Sometimes, there are days without sleep. Even while in school.

    Then suddenly, it's like something in her hated me. The mood would change. Making me afraid of her; I didn't feel like trying anymore. When I would wake up, and I would still be alive, I would cry all over again to say wow, God doesn't even want me. Now that I'm typing it, it's funny that I thought like that. One of my issues was that she never believed in me, let alone believed me. I wish she knew me. She became too invested in what I ruined rather than what I could have been if she had just taken the time to learn to love me. I thought my love for her was strong enough to fight for us. I learned a lot from her and my father, which has much to do with who I don't want to be and how I want to be treated or treat others. I consider both of them big blessings because God chose them to bring me closer to Him. I had to learn about myself from Him. It's not about where I came from but where I'm going. Life will always have difficulties, but it doesn't bother me because my eyes are focused on Jesus.

My DREAMS GROWING up

"God uses dreams to reveal, chastise, instruct, guide,
and lead His children"

Dreams are very significant but something we ignore. As a child, I didn't see it as something that made sense or had meaning. I would have so many dreams, and my dreams were so vivid. I had dreams of my dad right before I saw him for the first time after a long time, a time when I shouldn't have remembered him. I remember having this dream where I had to be 2 years old in the dream when cops came to the door with my mom to come and get me. I was on the steps with my diapers on, and I watched them take him. I knew exactly who he was when I saw him because of the dreams. A lot of my dreams were nightmares; I was constantly waking up crying.

There was this one dream I kept having; I was young, in the dreams, I was in Liberia, and even more scary was that I was naked, and a black figure was chasing me. The dream was so vivid that I would cry and scream, and in that dream, I would die. Every time, I would wake up crying, unable to explain or make sense of it, but I had this recurring dream up until I was in fourth grade. At times, most of my dreams were memories of things that had already happened but I never knew. The nightmares made me sleepwalk and talk while sleeping; it was so bad. One time, I was told I walked out on the street while sleeping and almost got hit by a car. I would have a flood of dreams that felt like real life. If I had a dream about something, it would happen. I've had dreams of people dying, and I remember one day, I had a dream of my grandmother's funeral, and at this funeral, I saw people marching with all black on from head to toe, their faces and everything covered; they were all going to her funeral, then when I woke up from the dream at that very moment my mom got a call, news from home that her mom just died. Once I heard her cry, I knew what it was because I just had that dream. The dreams were intense, and I also started having visions; I would see things but wasn't knowledgeable about the gift.

    I prayed never to have those dreams again because it was getting too accurate. After that prayer, I couldn't remember my dreams. The older I got, the more I realized the power and the gift of dreams God has given me; this scripture helped me know that my dreams were God's gift to reveal, to shed light, to instruct, to warn, and to give direction; *"In the last days,' God says, 'I will pour out My Spirit upon all people. Your sons and daughters will prophesy. Your young men will see visions, and your old men will dream dreams." Acts of the Apostles 2:17 NLT.* God speaks through dreams, and for a long time, I rejected most of those dreams, whether good or bad. Dreams, I later realized, can also be manipulated by the devil, and not all dreams are from God. I didn't understand them, so I rejected them.

The POWER of PRAYER

Prayer is the master key.

When I thought I was at the end of my rope, God heard me the entire time. Every tear I cried wasn't in vain. I remember crying so many times, asking God to take me just to avoid killing myself. I just wanted a painless death, something that would happen in my sleep while asleep. I wished and prayed to sleep and not wake up, to escape the madness all around me. I needed some peace in my heart, at least. My mind was often flooded with so many thoughts; I wanted my mind to shut down because I had so many thoughts racing through my mind. I couldn't control it anymore, and I felt like I would lose my mind. One night, I was lying on my bed, and I began to cry.

I told God that if He truly loves me and wants me to stay here, even though I don't want to live anymore. He should come down in human form to come and save me and show me that I'm capable of being loved. *"It's so hard being here; show me that You are here with me and can at least hear me."* I wept bitterly. I talked to Him the whole night, crying through my words. I asked Him why He placed me in a family that could care less if I died. I knew I was far from perfect, but I just wanted rest and peace of mind. I knew He was real, but I needed proof that I was a part of the ones He loved. I began to believe that if others didn't love me, how could He? I couldn't even love myself.

Right when I thought that was it, I went to Church the next day, not expecting to wake up. Believe it or not, I woke up more upset, like, wow, I'm still here. We had an altar call or something I had to come out for, and my pastor and her husband were praying for people individually. For some reason, I just wanted her to pray for me and no one else, and that is what was said in my head. When she got to me, she paused and began to cry. She held my hands and said God loves me very much. He told her to tell me that I am very beautiful and He wants to use me. She kept talking, and the more she spoke, the more she cried. And the more she cried, the more I cried. I didn't understand what was happening. I never cried in public. I was in disbelief at what was being said. That moment shook me. She always told me I reminded her of the daughter she lost, like there was something about me, something I carried, that I was powerful. Unbelievably, after that, it went through one ear and out the other. You would think that because I cried, I would change, but I didn't.

I forgot about the prayer and everything. I was even the President of the Youth Department in the Church at that time. I was so good at giving advice and being a motivational speaker about what God can do for you, but I couldn't accept it for myself. I knew what God could do for them, but I didn't believe God wanted it for me. I was living but with no motivation to live. It constantly became such an overwhelming feeling in my mind. It was annoying sometimes. Later, I was reminded of this prayer and how much God truly listened to every word I said. God knows what every single tear drop says.

I now understand that the shaking and breaking are for my making. He was making and molding me all along, even in the worst periods of my young life. Not long after, God sent me to His daughter, Queen Belema Abili, a woman who would eventually change my life. God sent me someone with whom I would experience Him in true form; He sent me a true mother to this generation. She is one of the best mothers I've ever encountered. My journey took me to Queen Belemzy Ministries -School of Power, where I've grown in many ways and finally learned what God's love truly means. The prayer was intentional, and God heard me. A lot of things that I prayed for, like God coming down to me in human form, was really to know that I was loved.

REPENTING *and* GIVING *my* LIFE *to* CHRIST

"There is no pit so deep that God's love is not deeper still."
— Corrie Ten Boom

When I thought my life was over, it was just beginning! I went to a few churches which I can count on hand throughout my life. Never really a home church besides the one I went to before my current church. A lot of them made me feel that church was just a building. I didn't want to even go near an African church at all; I feared prophets because I always felt like they could see through me and see what I've been through and would say it. So, I never want to see them or be around them. I even attended church with my dad's sister to sing backup for her daughters.

For me, African churches, back then, reeked of hypocrisy, a place to go show off your fancy cars and a parade of your new clothes, and once that show was over, I didn't want to be there. It didn't feel like a place you go to seek God. I didn't even know you had to seek the face of God in the first place. I didn't even read my Bible; I can't remember if I had one. I know I didn't. I couldn't even remember any messages preached or scriptures quoted. After being in that church for a while, we changed churches, and when I started going to our new church, it was much better than the old one because I picked up a Bible there. I was learning a lot, but I still wasn't listening. I would hear it, but I wouldn't be a doer of what I was hearing. I grew up in that church. Although I loved that church spiritually, it wasn't helping me. It felt like the beginning of where God was going to take me.

While we were still attending the other church, I heard my mom listen to this lady and laugh, and she didn't laugh often, so trust me, I noticed. Even when I tried to mind my business, I noticed that she and my stepdad said they were fasting one day, and I thought it was a joke. One day in 2018, my mom and stepdad told me about this Ministry they found on Facebook. My mom found it, not knowing she found it for me. When they first joined the Ministry, I didn't pay attention. I felt like it wasn't for me. But the way they began to change got my attention. The way they fasted and fell in love with God caught my attention. They were learning things and wanted to share what they've learned with people and not just keep it to themselves. They were also open about their feelings, which was new to me at least, so I got slightly intrigued. At first, I didn't understand fasting; I was confident it was not something I would ever do.

So, in the beginning, there were times when they were fasting, and I would eat. I used to say, "I thought Jesus was the only One who needed to fast. I'm trying to be like Jesus, not be Jesus, let me eat." One day, they said that they were going to a program and were going to be fasting. Let me say that they didn't even ask me if I wanted to go. I was told we were attending a program, but I had no choice. This was a three-day dry fast, and at first, I was like, yeah, I'm not doing that. Then I found myself fasting, and honestly, I thought I was going to die. I told God I didn't know what it was, but if He didn't see that I was really trying, then I don't know what to do next. When I came to Queen Belemzy Ministries - School of Power, I was about 20 years old and still trying to figure out my life.

I felt good about the Ministry, but initially, I felt like I was avoiding the truth about what God wanted to show me. There was something different. I had no clue if my life would change, but I wanted to see what the hype was about. I had to learn a lot about commitment and consistency. I wanted to see what would happen if I was truly invested. But once I made up my mind, there was no going back. I started changing a lot; some things were fast, and others much slower. I stopped wanting to be around certain types of people. Many people I hung around cussed a lot, and I was invested in that for so long that I had to get out of it. I didn't want to cuss anymore.

    I didn't want to talk about things that weren't Godly or about God. I loved my friends. I can still say that they are all amazing people. They changed my life. Things I considered little lies, masturbation, watching porn, all these sinful things, first I had to learn they were sinful to begin with. Then, most of them started dropping so quickly. I grew up in Philly, so many things we say have curse words. That was just the vocabulary I was used to, but I knew how to filter it in front of adults. Cussing was the hardest one, but it was the quickest to leave. Before coming to the Ministry, I knew some things were considered sins, but not many.

    I had no clue that I was a lukewarm Christian. I

thought I was an excellent example of what a "Good Christian" should be or act like. I thought being a good person would grant me access to Heaven automatically. Going to Baltimore, Maryland, in 2018 for my first program in the Ministry, I was in for the shock. The shock came from the fact that I fasted dry and then how she preached about God. I felt like I was walking through the chapters of the Bible. The way she had an understanding made you know this message was straight from Heaven. I had no clue what I was getting myself into.

    Although I wasn't one hundred percent, I knew in my heart that my efforts meant something to God. The more I watched her programs, the more I changed. The programs were twelve hours long but felt like one hour each time. At that program in Baltimore, I got delivered for the first time from the spirit of anger. At the one-on-one, I've never been so vulnerable enough to allow anything like that to happen. That's how powerful God is, though; I had no clue. Yeah, you hear stories or watch videos, and it feels like the people are faking. This one shocked me; I thought I was tough, but tears rushed from my eyes, which made me want to watch more. I was impressed; not even my mom could make me cry publicly.

The whole atmosphere of the house began to change. On our way home from that program, my mom apologized to me. I knew I needed to keep watching. After that program, I focused more on church and wanted to learn what my pastor was preaching. Talking to the youths was for more than just motivation; I would speak and get chills like I was meant to do it. I preached for the first time that year and was proud of myself. My first ever preaching video on Facebook came that year, and I couldn't believe I was even telling not just the church people but also the pastor of this Ministry online. Everyone wanted to know why the programs were so long, and I was happy to explain why. The way I talked about this Ministry, you would think I was there when it was created.

Change wasn't automatic; I didn't completely change overnight. When I turned twenty-one, I still went out to drink on my birthday. Then, when turning twenty-one sank in, my interest in things died down. Then God told us to move closer to the anointing where my stepdad would work for the Woman of God when I heard I had mixed emotions. What I grew up around was now about to change: the people, the food, and the environment. Let me not forget Houston didn't have a WAWA (a gas station with great food). If you know, you know.

Nonetheless, I was ready for the change; Philly began feeling toxic. My skin looked terrible; things were fighting the move; I almost burned down the house trying to use an air freshener. I nearly cut off my entire finger; every day, something was happening to me. I was over it and ready to get up out of there. I started losing friends right before the move. One of my closest friends and I were arguing over stuff that made no sense. It felt like a whole breakup, and I was sad. She will forever be my bro, but we did part ways. Eventually, we discussed it, and I even prayed for her and her mom. It was indeed a beautiful moment. We touched down in Houston, and everything was different.

I remember my mom said we had officially arrived in America. When I got there, I started school. I was supposed to end my senior year of community college, but I still didn't know what I wanted to do. I went to school and became a CNA, then again to become a MedTech. Shortly after, I started working in a nursing home, and I almost died there. What helped me was the fact that I was always at the School of Power studio. It was this peace that made me feel secure. It was like my peace of mind. I always wanted to be around Woman of God (Belema Abili). Being around her made me feel like I was in a different world.

She would talk to me about things, but I never told her what I was going through. She spoke of God a lot, and I loved that. She told me about my dress and how to carry myself better. Honestly, I like baggy clothes; I like comfort. Then again, my mom was my influence with clothes, so I wore much of what she got me. With my weight being all over the place, it was hard. When I noticed that tight clothes made men look at me, it made me like baggy clothes more. It worked sometimes, but only some of the time. I could only do that if I weren't with my parents. They considered it sloppy.

One day, we had a program in the studio, and I heard a voice, which I didn't often hear, a voice that I hadn't even heard before, and I knew it was God. He told me that when we were going up to share things, I should talk about how I used to be suicidal and depressed. That was the first time I publicly spoke up about things like that. Soon after that, learning to hear the voice of God and the things He would tell me to do, my relationship with Him got better, and I got closer to God. I began to learn about Him more and began to want to obey Him and do His will more. I didn't want to be the same me that I was before. We had a program in the studio again; this time, it was a 24-hour program. Within this program was the first time I heard God tell me to tell my Apostle that I was raped as a child. For the first time since I got saved, I rejected it. I was in disbelief that God would even ask me to say that because there was a part of me that I wasn't ready to open up about. Aside from that, I've buried the memories for a long time and didn't want to dig up those skeletons, not now or ever. I cried bitterly in the back office. While others were having encounters, and I was hearing that. I couldn't believe what I was hearing.

On March 1st, 2020, I told her, and when I told her I was so scared, I thought she would speak to my mom about it. We all know pastors who do that, even use it against you. Telling her I could feel my heart sink to my stomach. But she never did that; she never told my mom or anyone. Instead, she made me feel loved and protected. She told me later that she felt some way when I told her. I told her I felt like this was just one of those things she heard often. I had no clue it made her look at me differently. Although I told her, she knew we didn't talk much about it. She just always checked on me and asked me if I was okay.

And it made me love her even more. She was more than a destiny helper. She was like a mom straight from Heaven. I was so happy. My stepdad liked the idea of going to a physical church, so we even started going to her ex-spiritual father's church right before he got exposed as a voodoo priest by God. I hated that church—the fear I would feel just by being there. The youth department, choir, and everything were all over the place. It was nowhere near Queen's preaching. In his church, I felt God was mad at me; everything was harsh. Then, in hers, it was the Love of God from every angle. There was discipline but with Love.

My mom started drifting from God and the Ministry during the exposure. Although our relationship was never the best, she was trying. especially when she started getting closer to God. Suddenly, her priorities, friends, and everything started changing. She wanted to be a part of the world, and I was not going back. We weren't getting along at all. I didn't even want to be around her. Everything about her spirit irritated me, and that's how I knew we had different spirits.

The spirit in her did not like me. Just like before

we got saved, our relationship was not good because she hated me. I felt like I was reliving that moment all over again. This time, I wasn't having it. I wanted to leave, move out, be alone, and serve God. I told my Apostle about it, and she told me to pray for her. She told me to fast for her. She would put me on a three-day dry fasting along with my stepdad. That's when he talked about leaving and that he was starting to see other women as attractive, and I was shocked. I wanted to be alone, away from the drama, but this was different. All I could remember when we were fasting was constant arguments with her, and I would not talk because the fasting was dry. If the people in the back didn't read it, it was three days dry, with no food or water. It almost made me stop fasting.

I wanted to end it. She was being so rude all through the period. Then she got sick, and I was praying for her and interceding on her behalf, and asking God to have mercy on her, but she didn't care. She didn't want to pray or fast and said that my stepdad and I praying and fasting were enough for the whole family. Then I started having dreams of her dying and missing rapture. One night, I told her about a rapture dream bothering me. It all started with me getting very restless. God kept telling me to tell her the dream. I had to wait for her to get out of the shower. He told me he had a message for her. I waited and started praying, but my heart was racing. It was almost like if I didn't do it; I would be living in disobedience and punished for it. It was like a command. So I obeyed. I went to knock on her room door and told her. I expressed that I needed to tell her something.

The moment I started explaining the dream, I started to cry as if she had already died. I told her that she hears from God and she's not listening. The way God took over, the tears were overflowing. As I told her, I thought it would make her sit up. But instead, she shut me down. At that moment, she rebuked the dream and made it seem like my dream came out of the air. She said just because she's not praying, fasting, or watching like me does not mean she doesn't have a relationship with God and speaks to God in her own time. My face changed as if I was never crying. I just said okay and left the room. When I went to my room, I talked to God, saying that I did my part, but please help her. At that time, we had an assignment to explain what this Ministry had done for us and how it had changed us. Apostle was messaging me while the videos were live-streamed, and then she told me about my video. I need to look at the camera from now on when I speak.

I even discussed what had just happened with my mom. For my video, I previously had an Encounter where I met two people in one day. What made me anxious that day was a dream I had when I truly gave my life to Christ in the Ministry. It was a rapture dream where the setting looked like New York but desolate. I was in a black Jeep with papers in my hand; they were flying out of my hand. Then I was out of the car, panicking with tears. When I woke up, God told me those papers represented people and their salvation. I need to stop wasting time and tell people about Him before it's too late for them.

That morning, I was so restless that I could scream on the street to tell people to repent. On my way to school, I got in an Uber. After saying Hi, I asked, "Are you saved or Christian?" I'm not even sure why I even asked him that or even why I asked that question. He told me that if he is a Christian, then he is saved. And I told him no, that's not true. I told him that some people can be Christians and not be saved. So I asked him again, "Are you Christian, or are you saved?" he said yes to both. I continued asking him questions, and he began to tell me that he didn't believe that God speaks to His children and that there's no existence of hell. He said he doesn't believe that God's children are worthy enough for God to speak to us. So he doesn't believe when people say God just told them something. While this man was talking, it was like this anger was boiling in me. I felt like I was going to explode. He kept saying things, discarding who God is. As he talked, I asked God if this is how it feels when we reject Him. I wanted to cry; I wanted to scream; it was like something scratched my heart; it was almost like a heartbreak.

It hurt so bad I couldn't wait to leave the car. When I finally got to my destination, he said just because we don't believe in the same things doesn't mean we don't serve the same God the moment I close the door. It's like I heard that was his last chance. I remember hearing that he would die before he got home. I felt like I was living in my rapture dream, and I was sad throughout my entire class. I got another Uber to go home. This Uber driver was so excited, and it was different. That's when I encountered my first angel, Louis. So I explained all that in the video and about our fasting when the Woman of God said that the guy I spoke with was an angel. I was in shock. I was a little scared because I just said jokingly what if he was my angel and he was.

    My Apostle instructed me to call His name three times when I prayed later that night. The moment I began to do that, I started speaking in tongues, which was deep. God began to speak through me a message of repentance. The presence was so strong, the atmosphere was so heavy, and at one point, I became overwhelmed. I spoke in tongues for almost 3 hours along with talking. That had to be one of the most intense moments I've ever had with God. It changed a lot for me. People were making fun of me, saying I was going crazy. They even said that I was not there when I was in Philly. I took that motivation, and I began preaching on Instagram. I had a mini youth group, which was an experience I learned a lot from them. It made me know that God called me to speak to the youth, which my Apostle prophesied right before it happened. That assignment made me truly appreciate what my Apostle does for us daily.

    She works so hard that I've never seen anyone who works as hard as she does. When God told her to start preaching online, she allowed the Holy Spirit to help her. Her drive and love for God made her stay consistent, which is truly an inspiration. It made me confident to preach and even tell my life story to people online. I wanted God to be proud of me and pleased with me. I no longer cared what other people thought of me. Salvation is personal; no matter how much I may love a person, I'll never love them more than I love God. My morals differ; I want to be the best for God and myself. I have constantly watched my Apostle be in the presence of God without hesitation. It has molded me, so I can't afford to mess up with God. Following her, I could know when God was speaking from my mouth. I can discern. There are so many things in life I never discerned. I just went along with whatever flow I was around.

Working in the Nursing home brought me closer to God. There was so much going on in the atmosphere. On many occasions within the facility, I was attacked by the clients. They would be aggressive when I was trying to change their "depends" or get them into night clothes. After being attacked so many times, I eventually got fired. I felt like the system failed me. I did things how they told me to do them, but when it came to speaking the truth, they went mute. From that, I learned things don't always happen how we think. God's ways are not our ways. The same day after getting fired, my mom started yelling at me and blaming me for being fired. But my story didn't end there because God hired me to work for His anointed daughter. I was so happy, and I am still excited now. Before getting hired, I was already at the studio every day. I just loved being there, honestly.

When I got hired, it started from the day we went to the studio for a fasting we had. At first, my mom didn't allow me to go with my stepdad. She argued about my job situation and told me I was not going to the studio that day. When I was upstairs, I cried to God, and the next thing I knew, she started asking me if I was ready to go. I was shocked, but I was ready, lol. When we went, the Queen said I heard you got fired, but don't worry, God will favor you. You will also get another job so don't worry or be stressed. After the service, Queen's eyes were closed, and she asked me what I was good at, like what I could do in the studio. I was like, I can learn anything, like cleaning and anything I need to know. I was so happy. No, I was excited. Before I was officially hired, I was already working and had nothing to do.

This was in 2020. The day I got hired, we had a

meeting. She even told me about a dream of me holding her purse as she walked. I believe I either walked behind her. I was also having dreams before of me with her discussing important things and then one of me holding her wig. So after that conversation, she asked the other workers, "Do you guys like her? Is she a good fit?" and they said, "Yes."

I was super excited. I still feel the same way even today. Working with her, I'm always learning and still learning so much. I've learned so many things about myself working for Queen: I am productive, proactive, fast according to the pace of how I should be, and not timid but bold. Most of these things came from being rebuked a lot. It always came from a place of love and not hate. When someone wants the best for you, they will tell you so that you can do better, not keep quiet, for you to keep doing the same, and then eventually fail.

One of the biggest rebukes I got was when I went to London for the first time. I felt like the world froze. Imagine being fired in a whole different country. I was working during the program and recording at the same time. Suddenly, it's like confusion took place. At that moment, everything done was time-sensitive. God needed me to be fast, and I was not. That's when God publicly fired me. I felt like God had left me that day. Before that, I was on a fast, and God told me He would show me all the sides of His Love. Before we left, he assured me I knew He still loved me despite the rebuke. *"The Lord disciplines everyone He loves; He punishes everyone He accepts as a child." - Hebrews 12:6 ERV.*

Within that same program, I was restored back on the last day, just a few minutes before the program ended. It felt like I had just been accepted into Heaven, one of those moments you see on TV where everything is in slow motion when the confetti falls from the sky. I was so happy, a true joy. If Adam and Eve were restored, they would be as happy as I was. Many may not understand, but it's not for them to get; it was a lesson that became a message for me and others. That was one of the most challenging moments in my life concerning God showing me all the sides of His Love.

During the exposure time in the ministry, I was going through persecution within my household. This was a test, and I was not going to fail my test. We had assignments, and I would post as we got them and completed the assignment. Nobody would make me miss what God was doing and what He was about to do in my life. Many times, my mom and I argued a lot. One of the days I posted that the false prophet was a rapist, she came again saying that he never raped Apostle. I wanted to know how she knew and if she was there because she was too confident with her answer. What made me mad is that her words felt like she was saying it to me and coming from someone who has been raped.

When you look someone who has been raped in the eyes and call them a lair, it's like you never want to talk to them again. She even tried to hit me that day, and I looked at her, and I was ready. But the Holy Spirit told me to calm down, and I did, and I just walked away. As I walked up the stairs, I suddenly got a message from Queen telling me not to fight my mom or fight with her. I was shocked because it just happened. With that, we just walked past each other in the house for a while. It made that assignment very hard to do, but the fight was worth it. Even from this same argument, I got my first deliverance at a program my Apostle did.

Many things occurred over the years, and I became increasingly different from them. The thing is, I've always been an outsider. Getting saved just helped me define who I'm supposed to be. *"Don't copy the behavior and customs of this world, but let God transform you into a new person by changing the way you think. Then you will learn to know God's will for you, which is good and pleasing and perfect."* (Romans 12:2 NLT) I was happy to be different. I never wanted to stand out; I tried to blend in. I learned to fast for my mom and pray for her regardless of how I felt. It's not about us or how we feel. Think of it like this: we want to be like Jesus but don't want to love like Him. The way we portray the true spirit of God is by walking in His footsteps. This means praying for those who hate you and speak against you. For your Father in Heaven gives light to the good and the evil. Queen always helps me to understand that this life is bigger than feelings. Although the prayers helped, and my mom eventually came back. It didn't last long. Even with that, salvation is personal; no matter how much you may pray for someone, they still have to do their part. God wants to hear from them Himself.

    When Apostle Queen Belemzy got the instruction from God to move to Columbus, Ohio, I was ready for a fresh start. For it to be a fresh start, I had to be released of everything that could hold me back. After falling into a trap, God made me stay behind. Staying behind, I had a lot of self-reflection to do. I had to figure out what I wanted to do with my life. It was a test to see if I genuinely wanted to serve God with all my heart or bow. I knew what I wanted and where I wanted to be. I had to do a 17-day dry fasting and prayers on my own; many of the days that I was supposed to break, I never did. God didn't allow me to eat the food in the house, so I would wait until everyone was asleep to order Uber Eats. I never fasted before I came to the Ministry, but now, because I was ready for God to change my life and things needed to break, I had to give God the access He needed to move significantly in my life. I became depressed; it felt like God left me. I just wanted God to move in my life.

Since the altar was taken down without the consent of God or Apostle Queen Belemzy , we were all fired at that point. Although I was not a part of it, it was something God was doing, even if I didn't understand. I had many decisions to make, including what exactly I would be going back to school for. I did not want to do it, but because it was an instruction from God, I considered it with so many emotions and thoughts going in my head, feeling abandoned and rejected by God. It did not stop there because I had "the talk" waiting for me when I got home that day.

The day we got fired, my mom and stepdad felt it was the perfect time for them to talk with me.

They expressed how I haven't spoken or come down to be around them since the Apostle left. Even if I eat, it's just something small for me. I ate ramen noodles with boiled eggs and spam for the longest time. They said I needed to let them know my plans for school and life and if I even wanted to be there. My mom said if I didn't want to be there, I should know that I could leave and that no one was holding me back from going.

I sat there and allowed them to finish talking for almost an hour. I said my peace and left that table. After that, I stayed in the presence of God because I needed to understand what was happening. It felt like my life was falling apart. It was a constant argument because I wanted to stay in my room. On the days that I was supposed to break my fast, I didn't even eat. I didn't want to be around them; I just wanted to avoid any form of argument. When I ordered food via UberEATS, I had to wait until they were sleeping to get it. I would give special instructions to the delivery driver about where they should put the food so they wouldn't be seen on the camera for the house. It became so hard;

they started making all these rules. For example, when I was worshiping, I had to wait for my stepdad to be done studying. Or I needed to lower my worship music so that they could blast their music, which was worldly music.

Then, when their friends came over, it was a whole different thing. I started to feel how I felt when I wasn't saved. I kept saying to God that I felt like I was going to die in that house. What made me their enemy in the house was that I spoke the truth when my stepdad started exaggerating what happened. Still, to this day, I feel like God is the one that spoke from my mouth that day. They felt like I should have lied or not said anything. When what was being said was exaggerated. They constantly complained about me in the house, which became very tiring. I began to pray to God and ask Him to take me out of the house. That if He's pleased with me to show me for my last couple of days of my fasting. I needed peace that I was doing something right. Sometimes, my Apostle would message me to check up on me. She doesn't even know that's what God used to give me strength.

Since moving, Apostle Queen Belemzy was doing her first program in Columbus, Ohio. We officially started packing many things from the studio to take there. While the other workers did that, she asked me to run errands. It helped me get out of the house. I took some of her things with me to her parent's house. I was so weak, but I was happy to be there. She video-called me and her mom to see what we were packing for her. I had to stop myself from crying, so most of the time, I kept my head down. Later, she told me she would fly me out to Columbus, Ohio, for the program to work. Although we were fired, we were already paid for the month, so it was only fitting that we worked for the rest of the month. That was one of the days to break my fast. I took my time going home. I even went out to eat and relaxed my mind for a bit.

During that time, I stopped talking to my friends, so I felt alone and wouldn't even be able to explain how I felt. When I got home, it was like a war zone. My mom told me that she wanted to talk to me. Oh boy, that talk was something else. As soon as I walked through the door, she started talking about everything, including the fact that I just came home. My mom talked about many things; some didn't make sense. She told me that it's family over everything, that blood is thicker than water, and that we are supposed to stand up for each other. All I could remember thinking in my head was the scripture in the Bible when Jesus spoke about who His family was. *"Jesus replied, "Who is My mother? Who are My brothers?" Then He looked at those around Him and said, "Look, these are My mother and brothers. Anyone who does God's Will is My brother and sister and mother." Mark 3:33-35 NLT.* She said, "If Queen decides that she doesn't want me around again and I kill myself, then what?" What I am looking for is what I will get. That I don't know these people." When she was done, I told her I was going to Columbus for the program. She said if you choose to come back, don't expect to be welcomed back here. Don't think you have a home here waiting for you. As I went upstairs to pack, I packed my clothes like I didn't plan on returning. I didn't even ask God; I knew that was where my heart was. Where God wanted me to be. My heart wasn't with my mom in Houston or my dad in Delaware. I know that they knew at that moment that they lost me.

When I got to Columbus, Ohio, I knew I was home. I couldn't wait to be around my Apostle again; it felt like a decade since I had seen her. The program was terrific. God moved, and I even got a prophecy about going to nursing school. Within that prophecy, I was told that God heard my tears and that I would have CDs worldwide. She said that all the things I was facing were for the making of me. Once the program was over, the reality of returning home flooded my thoughts. I knew I had to return, but I wanted to end my fast in Columbus, Ohio. I needed God to show me something, so I dreamed of moving out. In the first dream, I was outside this huge house full of people. I was sitting on the steps with my friend.

In the house, I could hear them talking about me. I could see all the words flying in the air, and they were all words of hate and curses against me. The friend I was with I knew he was an angel or Jesus Himself, and as they were cursing me out and saying all kinds of things about me, I began to get angry. I wanted to storm into the house and give them a piece of my mind, but the angel told me to wait and not to say anything. When they settled down, I walked in, and inside the house, a light shined on me like a spotlight. When I got to the crowd of people, I saw so many faces, some I couldn't remember, but the one I remembered was my mom's face, and it was dark, almost unrecognizable (but I knew it was an evil spirit that took over her, not really her). I said, "I am 24 years old and moving out."

In the next dream, I went to the house in Houston to pack up my things. When I went to the house in the dream first, kids were pooping in my sink, just all over my room. In the first half of the dream, my Apostle came and told me which dresses and things I should take. In the dream, I made it clear that I just came to get a few things, picked out those things, and packed them. When I went outside, I thought my Apostle and one of my coworkers left me, which was God in the dream. But later on, I saw them, and I was so happy. In all these dreams, I did not see my mom being there at all. Like it happened in the dream, it happens in real life. When I woke up, I informed Queen of my dreams. When we discussed it, she told me to contact my parents and let them know what was happening and what was going on, especially regarding the dreams.

Even though I was a bit nervous. I made a group chat for both of them (my mom and stepdad), and I was very sincere and polite about the situation. I told them about school, my plans, and my plans to move out of the house. My mom said okay, and they also asked me when I would be coming. That same day, my Apostle helped me book a flight for me and my coworker to go and come back the same day. What I saw in my dream played out in real life when I went. When I returned, I knew it was time to get to business. I had to set goals, starting with getting an apartment and a good school. It was a bit of a struggle. School surprised me, but the apartment search was hard. Queen wanted the best for me, especially when it came to apartment searching, but God wanted to do something with me. We both had no clue what was coming.

When she released me, she gave me 10k, which was after the program. Ten thousand dollars, guys; I had to repeat it just in case you didn't read it the first time. We were still in the hotel for a little while after that, and then we found an Airbnb, but it only had room for three, so I knew I wouldn't be staying for long. When we were at Airbnb, I was apartment hunting and calling schools until I picked a school I was leaning toward. I couldn't find an apartment that fit my budget. At that time, I still didn't have a job. I was asking God how we were going to do this. Most of the time, Queen didn't like how they looked, so I even went to the one behind the Airbnb. That one was so expensive just for a studio apartment.

She even dreamed she was walking me outside

to my car, that my car was outside waiting. That was a way of God saying that I needed to be let go so He could give me the apartment He wanted me to have. We didn't pay any mind to the dream. Just for God to allow my mess up to be forcefully removed. I went live at a program without her being ready, and that day, I didn't know what pushed my hand. Coming home after that program, she told me I had to leave immediately. After packing my bags, I was dropped off at a hotel. I stayed in a hotel for a while, which was quite expensive. I was trying to rent a car and find an apartment. I almost got scammed with the car, but I eventually found an apartment that I never physically went to see. I just paid for it, along with a down payment. Then, I was approved. It was a little different from what I was used to, but I felt safe. It looked like drug dealers lived there, but because it's where God wanted me to be, I saw it as my castle.

    I had a lot of time to think while in the hotel. Most of the thinking had to do with reassurance of who God wants me to be rather than the thoughts I had that made me feel less of myself, voices that wouldn't get out of my head. I cried a lot; at times, it felt like God abandoned me, but at the same time, He was talking to me a lot. I had so many questions that I wanted to know what was happening. If I was even in His will or if I was on my own. The moment I got approved, I knew I was heading in the right direction. Before I even moved in, I remember my Apostle messaged me after I told her I got an apartment. I was so happy. She messaged me to check up on me. To ask me how things were going, I even told her about the car, which we both laughed about. I also sold my old car, which was in Houston.

She told me that God was doing something with me. Showing me that He is all that I need. Which is what He was doing with her at that time as well. She also told me many things to encourage me and make me stronger. It helped and made me strong-headed, and I needed it. I finally moved into my apartment and started school on March 30th, 2022. Glory, I was so excited. I took Uber everywhere; God did it for me and proved everything. I felt like I was spending money I didn't have. I had to start thinking of a job. Cleaning came to me first, then going back to work as a CNA, which was what I went to school for as well. I intended to work hard because failing was not an option.

One thing I'll always say I learned from Queen,

and I'm still learning, is her obedience to God and how that required hard work. Going to school became an assignment. Doing my best knowing that God and the Host of angels would be behind me, I studied a lot and had to focus more. Sometimes, my mind would be all over the place, and besides studying, I needed a job. Money was going to run out. I depended on Him to make a way; I applied every day. Then, I would remember the promises that God made me. The thought of being homeless came to me so many times. See, when you worry a lot, the devil feeds into it. He could put the thoughts, but you can reject it or entertain it. So many negative thoughts would flood my mind, and sometimes, I would have to take a break. With all of that, I'm glad that God allowed me to be able to hear Him. Especially in His Ministry, the messages feed me spiritually and emotionally. I knew I would be okay.

    Just when I thought all hope was lost, God led Apostle Queen Belemzy to message me to see her at the house (the Airbnb). Oh Lord, my heart was not only at peace; I believe I cried from how happy I was. I wasn't talking to my mom or dad; I disconnected from them but didn't block them, even my stepdad. It became a big thing. One day, when I was at the house with Queen, she was live, and we began to discuss what had happened thus far. The issue started when my mom came on the video intending to intimidate me. Making it seem like I was under a bad influence, she went on the video showing her true colors, even disrespecting Queen. With that, I was instantly disgusted by her and blocked not just her but her husband and my real dad. She spoke against my destiny helper, whom God sent to help me. It was bigger than that; I felt like she was disrespecting God. I prayed for them, but it wasn't the same. I wasn't even sure if I forgave them.

Queen allowed me to help her clean the house during that time and always blessed me with money, especially because she knew I wasn't working. Guess what, though? I would still worry. She would even ask me how much I have left in my savings. Making sure I would keep up with all my bills. She always wanted to make sure I was okay. The way she cared many times, I knew it was God caring for me through her. Whenever money would get low, I would panic; now I know I was worried for nothing. My spirit started rejecting the apartment, and I began having dreams.

Then I remembered Queen prophesied that I would get the apartment around where her new house would be. I believed. So, the day before my birthday (December 8th, 2022), God blessed me with a luxury apartment. I could not believe it because before God had Crowned me a princess, He had told me He would fight for me and that I was His Property. That's when things started falling into place, and it was so fast. I've never experienced this kind of love before. It was so overwhelming. God is so Good! It was a lot to me because I used to think I wasn't worthy of being loved by anyone. God did this for me. I didn't even like saying the words I love you. It used to be so hard to commit. I didn't want to be vulnerable with anyone, but sometimes I would be.

Because of God's blessings, I traveled with a Great and Mighty Servant Of God. I was chosen, and I had no clue. I was never put first, always last. God used His daughter to bless me with a brand-new car. Paid in full, not just a car that put me into debt. A car I never had to pay a dime for. That's not it. God didn't allow me to pay for the car insurance. God did that for me; my Apostle did it willingly. The true Heart of God. She never knew me before, but because God said it, she did it.

Many things happened within that time. I had

to reach out to my mom to make peace with her and my stepdad, letting them know that I forgave them. It took a lot out of me. I thought I forgave them when truly I didn't. I had no clue this was what God wanted me to do. When God wants you to do something, and you can't figure it out, you start making unnecessary mistakes you usually wouldn't make. All so you can be exactly where He wants you to be. I was so frustrated and confused. I felt like that was it. My Apostle blessed me with one thousand, and she paid for my ticket to go back to Columbus, Ohio, from Baltimore. I had to go to Houston the next day, so everything was handled. I first encountered my Apostle in Maryland, and my life began to change. So, I was excited to come back to thank God for where it all started. But God had other plans.

    I called my mom and my stepdad after unblocking her when I went. They didn't answer, but my mom called me back at the airport on my way to Columbus, Ohio. I was shocked at how well the conversation went. She was super lovely, saying things like she missed me. That she's proud of me. I was surprised at her words as I got on the plane; I even updated my Apostle on what was happening. When I got home, I started feeling a tsunami of emotions, and I didn't want to go anymore; I was asking God why I had to be the bigger person. During all this, I got a message from my Apostle, who showed me how my assignment to forgive became the message for the program in Baltimore. The message was her forgiving someone as well. I was encouraged, and I felt that I was ready. If she could do it, no doubt I could do it too.

Before getting to Houston, God spoke to me. He discussed with me how many days to stay, which was 2-3 days, depending on how it went. When I got to my hotel in Houston, Texas, I heard in my spirit that I needed to call my mom. When I called her, my mom added my stepdad to the call. Her whole mood went from "I miss you." to "What are you doing in Houston if you guys have a program in Baltimore?" I wasn't surprised, but I wanted to be. I hoped she changed, but it was the same old behavior.

The way she spoke, I knew pride and anger had overpowered her and him. God had to help me stay on that call. The amount of things that was said on that call I wanted to respond to, but I didn't. I just muted the call and let her talk, and then eventually, he spoke as well. I apologized if I hurt them in any way. I knew that it needed to be done. Many things she said were bragging that they now have so much freedom to do many things. They didn't think this was what I would be calling about. Listening to the call brought back memories of why I used to pray to be taken. One is that I felt like I was a huge burden to all of them. I no longer felt the pain. I just wanted to pray for them. Sometimes, people give off the impression that they have it all together.

Often, it's a cry out for help; I told them about a previous dream I had of them, which was scary. I knew I was obeying God by saying it. I felt like they would listen, but it made them angry. She said many things about what a birth mother should do, but when it comes down to being a mother to me, she wasn't that. It grieved me a lot. I chose myself, which meant choosing God. With God, I knew I learned how a mother loves her child. I prayed from my heart that someday she would have the child she always wanted, the one she would truly pour all her love into. Believe it or not, I love them and want the best for all of them, even my dad. They did what they felt was their best, even if they didn't try. They were more than blessed to be the ones to be my biological parents. God chose them. Someday, they will look and be glad He chose them.

I was a gift they didn't see before, but now, even if it's too late, they were once blessed beyond their expectations. I forgave from my heart, and God restored all my gifts and more. All because of forgiveness, which we don't see as necessary, but to God, it is. I even took the time to forgive even my rapist and everyone that hurt me and then the ones I hurt as well. I prayed that they would forgive me. We get hurt, but there are people that we have hurt knowingly or unknowingly. For instance, how we hurt God a lot when we sin or were even once sinners. Many of us repent daily, but God forgives us effortlessly, and I want to be just like Him. We must know that no one is perfect; we strive to be more like Christ.

A NEW CREATURE

"Therefore if any man be in Christ, he is a new creature: old things are passed away; behold, all things are become new." 2 Corinthians 5:17 KJV.

It took me a long time to get here, and it's the best place I've ever been. If this is where my story ends, I've made a significant impact; many will learn from my story. That suffering isn't the end. Jesus suffered for us to be saved, and in the end, He was and is still victorious, sitting at the right hand of God. Everything we go through is a build-up for the mass production of our extraordinary life story. I couldn't even believe I'd made it this far. It has indeed been a journey I am still on, and I love every moment. At times, I do have questions because, for a fact, it does get hard, so hard, but God always has a way of coming through. God has given me the great honor of serving His daughter, who is an excellent example of Him. It's one job that doesn't feel like a job but a lifestyle. It's so much a part of me that I don't see myself doing anything else that doesn't involve God.

I never even imagined working for God or being a servant of God; then, I remembered asking God to show me His purpose for my life here on earth. Every day, He's showing me that He didn't make a mistake putting me on earth. I've never been so grateful to be alive. My life has changed since I came to Queen Belemzy Ministries - School of Power. It has given me the will to live and to want more for myself, and being here, I know that God wants more for me. *"For I know the plans I have for you," says the Lord. "They are plans for good and not for disaster, to give you a future and a hope." Jeremiah 29:11 NLT*

I've experienced a love I never knew existed. So I thank God for my Apostle Queen Belemzy for being the one God chose to help change my life completely. One of my assignments here on earth is to tell people about His daughters' Ministry that has saved me, the place where Jesus planted me. Telling people is something I could do with my eyes closed. Queen Belemzy Ministries -School of Power is where lives change right before your eyes. I am a living testimony.

After being ashamed of how I sang my whole life, I finally came out of my shell and began to sing more. I proudly have released many songs on YouTube with the help of God and my Apostle. I'm not shy about singing how I want anymore. I now sing to the Glory of God because my Apostle always pushes the best out of me. I'm still learning every day to Love myself. With that, God broke down to me the way He felt when people hate themselves or even are suicidal. How sad it makes Him. Imagine Him taking His time and effort to perfect what He knew was good, something we are humanly unable to create. We want to destroy it all because we don't understand the importance of how special we are to Him.

    I am proud of the woman I am becoming. I want people to know how much they are loved. I feel so much better about myself. God never makes mistakes, and He never will. People said a lot about me when I got saved; they laughed at me and thought I was putting on a show. The high I was on with God, I didn't care. That's the thing: people will always have something to say. Nothing could stop me. I knew that if they experienced what I did, instead of talking about me, they would ask how I got there. They will talk even when you tell your story, but guess what? They aren't the ones living your life. They only know what you allow them to see. Losing people you thought would never leave you can be very humbling. You learn what Jesus meant when He was harsh against the people once they stopped getting what they wanted from Him. Not everyone around you is rooting for you. Getting closer to God opened my eyes to a lot. When I heard what everyone was talking about, they said that I'm Holy Mary now, possibly the funniest one.

    I have changed more than I ever thought I could have. That's what happens when you get saved. When you give your life to Christ, you will change. It helped me grow and be a better person. How I speak, dress, think, pray, or read is different. The advice I even give is beyond my years. The knowledge I have indeed come from God. The importance of being chosen is overwhelmingly beautiful, and a great honor to work for a servant of God. She is the best teacher; she preaches the words that come straight from Heaven like they are her last words. Every word leaves a mark, and she's a great example of living and serving God with your whole heart. She makes this life worth living, and I love her for it. She has indeed been a blessing to me.

    Even now, I stopped wearing glasses after years of wearing them. I have worn glasses for almost half my life. I was supposed to start wearing them in elementary school, but I started wearing them in high school. With the delay in getting glasses, my eyes got worse over time. They thought I was faking, not being able to see clearly. After that, God told me to stop wearing contacts, which almost made me blind. They made it a requirement to wear them even when I'm driving; never should I drive without them. On August 9th, 2023, I had a dream, and in this dream, I was driving with no glasses. Then I woke up with a message from my Apostle wanting to tell me something. When she called, she told us she could see, although it wasn't 100%. The more she testified, the more she could see clearer.

    The moment she started talking, I began to cry because I knew how bad her eyes used to be. Then I remembered my dream. I began to think that if she received the healing for this, so would I. Lo and behold, when I went to her house, I felt like I could see what she was seeing without my glasses. Stepping out on faith, I took my glasses off and things I could never see without my glasses. I could now see better; I was in disbelief. I was so joyful that it made me want to cry instantly. I don't like being emotional, but I just knelt to praise God when I went outside. Since then, I've been driving for a month without my glasses, which the doctor said I could never do, but God did for me! Hallelujah!! God is so faithful; I will never stop being loyal to Him. For He first loved me.

My dreams increased, and they are now super prophetic. Coming from someone who was always having nightmares, sleepwalking, and talking to now sleeping peacefully, having beautiful visions with Jesus and me following His footsteps. I have dreams of preaching on the street. Yes, I now preach on the street, starting from Instagram. I feel at home. When I preach on the street, it feels like I was born to do it. I would have known none of this if I had never come to His Ministry and been spotlighted. I have never been spotlighted anywhere like this before. It's an honor. I can now see clearly, spiritually and physically, in Jesus's name.

TELLING *my* STORY

"Everyone has a story, a message the world desperately wants to hear."

I wanted this part of the story to have its section, although it's almost last; it's what started this whole story. It happened in the most precious way. With grace, I told my story on Queen's platform of how I was molested as a child. Before I told my story, I was having such a tough time. My mind and my heart were closing in on me. I didn't think I could hold this secret any longer. I started having flashbacks of being molested whenever I would close my eyes. Things I didn't remember, I was remembering, and I couldn't handle it. I felt like I was losing my mind; I was struggling to breathe again like someone was drowning me.

    Then, I had this dream of people forcefully trying to take me away from my woman of God. I told her of the dream, and she told me not to worry. She was so sure that I would be okay. That same day, I went on some errands and later went to her house. When I went to her home that day, she was about to go live. So I came and dropped off what she needed and left the room, which was God's room, in her parent's house. Suddenly, I felt a rush of heat. Then I had a strange feeling like I needed to leave the house ASAP, but right before I could, she said Alexis, come to my room. When I got upstairs, she spoke to me for a little bit. We talked about the dream, but she could instantly see something was wrong. She said, I'll pray for you, but she was about to go live. Queen was the only adult I was ever comfortable telling my story to. At first, I thought she would tell my parents when she found out, but she kept it a secret and did not treat me any differently except to love me more than my scars.

She played a video, then she started to pray for me. As she prayed, she told me that I was free from the spirit of rape and many things, and I just felt this huge relief. I just broke down crying and couldn't breathe. She told me it was time to tell my mom, but I could feel it. I knew it was time. I was a little nervous because I had dreams of telling my mom my story, and she denied it ever happened. She didn't believe me, so I told her through a text message instead of talking face-to-face. Queen helped me write the message. I wrote it, and she approved it. She just told me to allow God to lead me while I write. When my mom got the message, she didn't respond immediately.

When she got home, she told me she made a group chat and forwarded my message. They wanted us to meet with her older brother and my stepdad when they came home. I didn't care for the meeting because her brother talked most of the time (not the one who molested me). He was pointing out the fact that he didn't ever touch me and always saw me as his child, which wasn't even relevant. Not too long after that, Queen messaged me because she was still live during that time, and we were even fasting. She asked me, "When do I want to speak about it?" I said, "I can do it whenever I'm ready." She then asked me, "How about today?" when I said yes, she told me to prepare. This was June 4th, 2021. When I came to the live that day, I felt liberated and powerful; I spoke about everything and even things I forgot I talked about on my live on Instagram. I was so grateful and still am because I have been beyond blessed since then. My mom's sister was blowing up my phone non-stop, and I had to block her. When you publicly expose them, they sometimes try to cover themselves up. Not with this one. Enough is enough. One thing I did do is forgive them.

Queen prophesied that I would write books and be a blessing to many. She said many other things, which I believe with every bone in my body. Even when my mom got the courage to talk to me again about my story, she still didn't know what to say. She said it was hard to digest and that I shouldn't blame myself for what they did to me. When I wanted to write a police report and asked for her sibling's information, she told me that I already exposed them. That's when I knew how she truly felt.

My aunt's husband called, and he said, "Did his wife say she molested me, or are they just going based on what I said to them?" When I heard that, I was shocked. I even remember my mom saying that day that whatever I decided to do, she would support me. They needed to go to jail, but she changed her mind the moment she kept talking to them. She asked me if I was ready to talk to them when she would speak to them, like, huh? That's when she told us that she was a victim of rape. Still, until today, this subject has been a little touchy for me because I can't believe I have made it this far. Jesus loves me. Imagine Him sacrificing His life for me to be saved. Someone that people didn't see as worthy is now worthy because Jesus made me worthy.

I want to leave this with you: no matter how hard it may be to tell your story, know that there is someone or even many out there who have a similar story to yours waiting for you to tell it. Waiting for someone to let them know that they are not alone regardless of how far God may seem from you, trust me when I say He is always hovering over you, waiting for you to give Him access. He can't fully take over if you don't let Him in. Look at me; I spent most of my life building this wall that only I could tear down. I had to choose to ask Him to help me.

Think of it like this: you are drowning in an ocean, and everyone is watching you; you need help, but none of them can help you, and the only One reaching out their hand to save you is God. Your only job is to reach back. That choice right there belongs to you. See, He is always there; you must try to meet Him, and He will guide you. The only way to do that is to repent. You are giving all the heavy burden you've been carrying for so long. Trying to be your own protector is exhausting; you're already at the point of giving up. Allow God to help you; give Him this chance to prove He's the best fit for this job. If you are ready to give your life to Christ now, say this salvation prayer after me:

Father, Lord, I come into Your Presence as a sinner.
I confess all my sins.
Please forgive me.
I didn't know any better.
I promise not to go back to my old ways.
I believe that Jesus Christ came and died for me.
On the Cross of Calvary,
So that my sins could be wiped away.
I accept Jesus Christ as my Lord and Personal Savior.
Be the Lord over my Life.
I promise to serve You forever and ever.
Amen.

Now put your hand on your chest and say, "I Am Saved!" Go and Sin no more.

The Bible says: *"And when people escape from the wickedness of the world by knowing our Lord and Savior Jesus Christ and then get tangled up and enslaved by sin again, they are worse off than before." 2 Peter 2:20*

NLT. Just as you have said, this salvation prayer, the person you were before has died and gone. Go and live your new life in Christ.

"Once you were dead because of your disobedience and your many sins. You used to live in sin, just like the rest of the world, obeying the devil—the commander of the powers in the unseen world. He is the spirit at work in the hearts of those who refuse to obey God. All of us used to live that way, following the passionate desires and inclinations of our sinful nature. By our very nature we were subject to God's anger, just like everyone else. that even though we were dead because of our sins, he gave us life when he raised Christ from the dead. (Only by God's grace have you been saved!) For He raised us from the dead along with Christ and seated us with Him in the heavenly realms because we are united with Christ Jesus. So God can point to us in all future ages as examples of the incredible wealth of his grace and kindness toward us, as shown in all he has done for us who are united with Christ Jesus. God saved you by his grace when you believed. And you can't take credit for this; it is a gift from God. Salvation is not a reward for our good deeds, so none of us can boast about it. For we are God's masterpiece. He has created us anew in

Christ Jesus, so we can do the good things he planned for us long ago." Ephesians 2:1-3, 5-10 NLT

    Let me tell you how imperfect I am or was. I hated God because I couldn't believe He would allow all of this to happen to me. I felt like He just watched, and He didn't care. I was like an Israelite; I was blinded by what I thought. I couldn't see from His point of view. The suffering was for a greater purpose that was beyond me. I can't believe I even thought of hating Him. Jesus was sent to die for me, a sinner, just to be saved. I know it's hard right now, and it seems like life is against you. I was there before, so I know. I want you to know that God is about to do something big in your life. Your suffering is not for nothing. I've gone through endless deliverance, and I'm still being delivered from things I didn't know I needed deliverance from or even existed. This all took place in Queen Belemzy Ministries- School of Power. God is about to shame the devil and show him you will be victorious. Believe that greater is coming. You will elevate, and life will not pass you by.

    When this happens, don't forget that God saved you. Don't forget to give Him all the Glory. Let people know who saved you, and do it boldly. Just because I don't fall into the same traps as you doesn't mean my story is better than yours or that I'm better than you. The number of times I was raped, I could have died, I could have gotten pregnant, or even gotten diseases that I would still be living with today. I survived not because I was worthy but because God had mercy on me. His Love protected me. I was far from perfect; I didn't even repent, and He was looking out for me. I didn't even know Him, but He knew me. God has been watching over me my whole life, and I did nothing to deserve it. I want it to be understood that I don't deserve this love, and many of us don't. Daily falling for sin without care, recklessly breaking God's heart, and He still sent His Son, Jesus Christ, to die for us.

"But people are counted as righteous, not because of their work, but because of their faith in God who forgives sinners." Romans 4:5 NLT

You should thank God you lived when everything in you wanted you to die. Thank Him for accepting you when you didn't accept yourself. It would not be right if I didn't acknowledge God in this big testimony. I read Romans from Chapters 1-4 and began to cry; our stories are relevant because Jesus Christ made them relevant. After reading my story, you should think of all the good things in your life. I have many good days, but the bad outweighs the good; for those good days, I am so grateful. But honestly, I am even more thankful for the bad days because they added more seasoning to my story. So thank God for everything. He is a great God. The moment I gave Him a chance, my life changed forever; everything gradually fell and is still falling off.

A MESSAGE from my HEART

You may be wondering how my life turned out now. In 2024, I finally traveled to Liberia, where my biological parents are from. A place I said I would never go, and I loved every moment of it. I got to pray on the land and take my destiny back. The Bible says I shall not die but declare the works of the Lord. Making that trip to Liberia was all possible because of my Apostle; all expenses were paid, and I'm so grateful. Then, I also got the courage to file a police report on my predators. With that, I got a call back from the detective, and I just know God is about to work wonders in my life. I'm not as close with my mom again. As God leads, I occasionally respond to her messages or, if it's her birthday, wish her a happy birthday, and that's it.

As for my mom and me, we both prayed to God and got what we prayed for. I love both of my parents. I pray for her a lot, and I know God will continue to watch over her—the same with my dad. I had to make a choice, and I made it for myself. The deliverances and my wanting to stay saved helped me a lot. I prayed, and God answered in a way I never thought of. God is amazing. I know you won't regret it. I just feel so much peace. I love how Jesus is changing my life and creating in me a clean heart. I know how I felt when I wasn't saved, and it's only something me and God knew. People may read this, and I think I have it all together, but I'm still learning. God is helping me. I started a podcast, and I'm just in awe God has changed my story.

Decisions are always challenging to make, but they are worth it. I won't be the person to lie to you and say it's so easy. I had to give up a lot. I had to commit to God that I would never turn back. Sometimes, there are tears, rarely of sadness, but there are tears during the journey to the new person I am in Christ. Remember that when it's hard, only God can see you throughseek Him; it's worth it. My heart is joyful, and my story continues, but it's entirely in Christ this time. Thank You Jesus!

Author's Note

Your STORY can BECOME a GREAT MESSAGE

And they overcame him by the blood of the Lamb, and by the word of their testimony; and they loved not their lives unto the death. Revelation 12:11 KJV

Remember, your personal journey holds the power to inspire and uplift others. Your story, with its trials and triumphs, has the potential to resonate with those facing similar challenges. Embrace that your experiences can be a beacon of hope, showing others they are not alone. Through sharing your story, you transform it into a powerful message of resilience, courage, and the possibility of positive change. As the Bible verse in *Revelation 12:11 KJV says, 'and they overcame Him by the blood of the Lamb, and by the word of their testimony; and they loved not their lives unto the death.'* This verse reminds us of the power of sharing our stories and how it can help us overcome challenges and inspire others. Your voice matters, and your story can be a source of strength for those who need it most. Embrace the opportunity to make a difference with the story that only you can tell. Despite your past, God still single-handedly picked you to tell that story.

LETTER *to* GOD

Dear God,

Thank You. I don't know what to say but thank You Father for sending Your only Begotten Son to die for me. I am so grateful. Only You know the journey we have been through to get here. I cannot complete this book without giving you the Highest Honor and Praise because You alone deserve the Glory. I remember the nights I cried bitterly saying that You hate me. Or even hating You because I felt like You were just keeping me in this world to punish me. People don't see cry often but You saw me cry almost every night. I barely slept, sometimes being overwhelmed. There's things I've said to You or even ignored You and sometimes I think of that cry. The mercy of You God is great. The way You loved me when I didn't love myself. You looked out for me, protected me, sheltered me endlessly. All I can and know to do is to Thank You. Never in my life did I think I would love You like this. You gave me the Holy Spirit and I want to thank You for the Holy Spirit as well. When I just sit and think of how You created me. Taking Your time to perfect me. Sometimes I didn't appreciate it but You God still never left me. You have made my life so great. So beautiful. All I can do is say Thank You. Speaking from my mouth, even speaking to me to the point I know Your voice. Wow. I really feel so special and I am grateful. You surrounded me with love. With everything that has happened to me You blessed me in all my pain. I could do this all day but I'll stop here for now.

SPECIAL APPRECIATION

Dear Apostle Queen Belemzy,
I wanted to take this time to make a whole page or even more dedicated to the woman God sent to save me. God is the reason for this honor, so I want to honor the God that lives within you. God knew what He was doing when He sent me to your Ministry. You are genuinely a God-sent. I want you to know how much of a blessing you have been to me; you are the definition of a prayer answered. Everything I've ever prayed for, I've seen happen for me in this Ministry. Whenever I think of all you have done for me willingly, I start crying; you have availed yourself for God to showcase His Love to His people. I want to tell you that even if I have to say it with my last breath, I want the world to know that God, yes, the Father of Jesus Christ, used you (Apostle Queen Belemzy) to save my life.

I've never had anyone love me like this. I am alive today because you let God use you. You are the best mother in the world. I have watched you love not just with your heart but your spirit. I can't begin to thank you for every message, preaching, prophecy, hug, and so much more. Thank you, Queen, for loving me and believing in me. May your blessing triple from how blessed I feel. I pray that God never stops blessing you. I am so proud to be a part of your Ministry, life, and family. Thank you for never leaving me; instead, you motivated me. God used you to take me around the world to places I've never dreamed of. I've been to London multiple times, Canada, Germany, Cyprus, Jamaica once or twice, Singapore, Liberia, Kenya, Mexico, and many different states within America that are uncountable.

I'm so happy to see you grow and elevate to greater and higher grace. Thank you for teaching me never to give up. You work so hard, and I know all your hard work will pay off—especially all the work and effort you put into me. Your support means the world to me, the way you check up on me. It might not be that big of a deal to other people, but it means the world to me. You make me so happy. I love laughing, crying, and mocking false prophets with you. The list could go on forever. You told me that God doesn't make mistakes. If I were loved the way I wanted, I would never serve God the way I do, and you wouldn't have me to work for you. I want to thank you sincerely. You helped me see that even if it doesn't come easy, that blessing that belongs to you will always come to you. Because of you, I will obey God until the end and work until God tells me that's enough. I will obey God until my last breath. That's what you teach, being faithful to God no matter what.

You have always seen the best in me, even when I didn't. Wow, you have motivated me in ways I cannot explain. You're like a well that doesn't run dry. The more I'm around you, the more I draw from it. The more I'm blessed. You have always looked out for me. When I moved, you made sure I didn't suffer anything you encountered in the past. You have treated me more like your child, which has helped me be stronger. Even with that, although I'm not your biological daughter, the way you have loved me makes me feel like I am. Your happiness for my growth made me want to grow more. My story has so much meaning because you were the first adult I spoke to, and that didn't make me feel like it was my fault. You let me know that it wasn't something that was supposed to happen to me, that those people were supposed to love me.

You helped me to forgive. Forgiveness is forgiving

the person because the devil is just using bodies available to him. This Ministry carries the power of life. It makes you want to live to see where God will take you. A joy that makes your heart glad. Know for sure God really loves you and gives you the best. Apostle Queen Belemzy once said everything is calculated to help somebody. That somebody is me. I asked God to show me that He loves me, and He gave me the best. You constantly give your time for people like me worldwide to be blessed. You have helped make my life beautiful by obeying God.

Wow! You have been a protector to me. I could write a book about how grateful I am that God created you and blessed me with you. God Bless You, Apostle Queen Belemzy. I love you so much. I don't know how to thank you without thanking God first. I have been and will always be truly blessed and thankful for my salvation. With God's permission, I will even thank Him for you in Heaven. Your work will never be in vain.

ABOUT *the* AUTHOR

Alexis Beloved is a Child of God. Crowned by God as His Princess, she is now known as Princess Alexis Beloved. She is a born-again woman after God's own heart, filled with the Spirit of God not only to serve but to be a voice for many who are raped, suicidal, and depressed victims. Following in the steps of her Apostle, as she follows Jesus Christ, she has found a new reason to live, and it has a lot to do with getting other lives saved as God has saved hers. I am here to make Jesus famous and show many that Jesus truly is the One who saves.

Social Media Accounts:
Instagram: @ihaveavoice_alexis
Facebook: Alexis Beloved
TikTok: @ihaveavoice_alexis
YouTube: Princess Alexis Beloved TV
Podcast(YouTube): Saving Lives with Jesus
SoundCloud: Princess Alexis

www.ingramcontent.com/pod-product-compliance
Lightning Source LLC
Chambersburg PA
CBHW050858240426
43673CB00009B/279